be

HERE

be
HERE

His Holiness the Dalai Lama

as told to Noriyuki Ueda

Portrait of the Dalai Lama created by vectorportal.com

Hampton Roads Publishing Company, Inc.
Charlottesville, VA 22906

Distributed by Red Wheel/Weiser, LLC

www.redwheelweiser.com

Sign up for our newsletter and special offers by going to
www.redwheelweiser.com/newsletter.

ISBN: 978-1-64297-014-2

Library of Congress Control Number
available upon request

Printed in the United States of America
BP
10 9 8 7 6 5 4 3 2 1

Publisher's note:

Attachment. Emptiness. Compassion. Existence. You will hear these words again and again in the teachings of the Dalai Lama presented in this book of wisdom.

Many buddhist practices and meditations focus on "being in the present moment." But what does that really mean? What does it mean to *be here now?*

The Dalai Lama speaks of attachment—to things, to people, to memory, to feelings of anger and resentment, to future goals. Being attached means we are not *here* now; rather, we are living through wherever our attachment takes us.

Emptiness. Does that mean we let go of everyting? Even the present thoughts in our minds? How does understanding emptiness help us to *be here now*?

The Dalai Lama is clear: if we are not educated about past history and if we have no sense of the future, then how can we possibly have a "present"?

In this wide-ranging discussion, the Dalai Lama talks about the nature of emptiness, compassion, and attachment—all toward the goal of telling us:

"Be here."

When we are here, we can practice compassion in the present moment and focus on social jusice *now*. When we are here, we are no longer attached to our past, no longer stressed about the future, no longer tethered to suffering.

Being here means we find happiness, peace, and the fullness of life.

• • •

This book was compiled from an interview with the Dalai Lama conducted by Noriyuki Ueda, a well-known Japanese author, lecturer, and cultural anthropologist. As a visiting research fellow at the Center for Buddhist Studies at Stanford University, he taught a twenty-part lecture series on contemporary Buddhism during which his students questioned him: "Can buddhism respond to contemporary problems?"

His interview with the Dalai Lama provides insight into the answer.

BE HERE

The time when only monks decide how we should practice Buddhism is over. People from all walks of life—educators, scientists, administrators—should come together to discuss the revival of Buddhism in our modern time.

The Buddha's teachings have two levels, wisdom and expedient means—or, in other words, the understanding of truth and practical action in the *here and now*.

"Wisdom" is the knowledge of causality, or emptiness; "expedient" refers to nonviolent action, or the practice of compassion.

What is emptiness? It is the view that all phenomena must be understood as mutually interdependent. This idea forms the core of Nagarjuna's teaching of the "middle way." Nothing arises without a cause.

This is in contrast to the Christian belief in a divine creator of all things. In Buddhism we grasp that all things are produced through cause and effect. Happiness, suffering, and all phenomena arise due to specific causes. All things are born not of themselves but from their causes.

Causality refers to all things being interdependent. Emptiness is not nothingness; it means that all things exist within causality. *All things are empty of self-nature; they*

"THE BUDDHA'S TEACHINGS

HAVE TWO LEVELS—

THE UNDERSTANDING OF TRUTH

AND PRACTICAL ACTION IN THE

HERE AND NOW."

do not exist on their own, but are mutually interdependent.

In Buddhism, both the wisdom of emptiness and the practice of compassion are important. Compassion and kindness are the essence of Buddhism.

Emptiness and Compassion

What is the connection between emptiness and compassion? Some Buddhist monks understand and expound the doctrine of emptiness, yet clearly lack compassion toward suffering sentient beings. In this case, there may be understanding of truth but no practical action.

If a person truly understands emptiness, then compassion naturally arises, and if it does not, then his understanding of emptiness may be flawed.

Emptiness means that all things are interdependent, yet it is often misinterpreted as nothingness. If we develop our under-

"IF A PERSON TRULY
UNDERSTANDS EMPTINESS,
THEN COMPASSION
NATURALLY ARISES."

standing of emptiness, then compassion naturally arises because all things are interdependent and interconnected in causality.

Yet how is it that compassion naturally arises? I think this matter conceals a very delicate problem.

Regarding the understanding of emptiness, there are four philosophical schools: the Sarvâstivāda, Sautrāntika, Yogâcāra, and Madhyamaka. The first two are Hīnayāna philosophies, and the latter two are independent Mahāyāna philosophies; those who study Mahāyāna Buddhism must study all four. The fourth, the Madhyamaka, is further divided into the Svātantrika and Prāsangika schools.

To understand profound emptiness, we must grasp the subtle difference among the views of "no-self" that is emphasized in the Yogâcāra, Svātantrika, and Prāsangika schools. The most profound and highest emptiness, according to the Prāsangika school, is the interpretation that all things exist depending on causes and conditions.

In other words, nothing exists on its own, but rather, existence is understood in such a way that all things arise dependent on causes and conditions. In this view of causality, all things are dependent on other things, and through causality we can perceive reality.

Emptiness is understood as causality. When we see that emptiness is based on causal-

"ALL THINGS EXIST

DEPENDING ON CAUSES

AND CONDITIONS."

"ALL THINGS ARE DEPENDENT

ON OTHER THINGS.

THROUGH CAUSALITY

WE PERCEIVE REALITY."

ity, then emptiness does not signify a void in which nothing tangible exists, but rather that all things arise in this world according to cause and effect.

My first point is this understanding of emptiness based on causality, in which nothing possesses self-nature. But the mind of compassion does not arise from this understanding alone.

My second point is that once we know the meaning of emptiness based on causality, we are able to see that the suffering of all living things is rooted in the mind of ignorance, and that it is possible to extinguish that ignorance.

Emptiness and ignorance are completely contrary to each other. The failure to understand emptiness and interdependence is ignorance, and as one strengthens one's conviction about emptiness, the mind of ignorance loses its power.

Through cultivating this awareness of emptiness, the ignorance that is the source of our confusion and suffering can be extinguished.

We see that sentient beings suffer because of that ignorance, and a feeling of compassion toward them arises. We become able to see the cause of human suffering. We see that if we extinguish its cause, suffering disappears, and that is how compassion arises.

There are many different levels of understanding of emptiness, but if we correctly perceive the most profound emptiness based on the teachings of the Prāsangika school, then we know that ignorance can be cleared away. When we see sentient beings suffering because of ignorance, the mind of compassion awakens in us.

For monks who study profound sutras and achieve a high level of knowledge, it is difficult for them to feel compassion toward ordinary suffering because their knowledge is academic.

According to Buddhism, human beings experience three types of suffering: the suffering of physical pain, the suffering of change, and all-pervasive suffering.

Of the three, the studied monks tend to be more aware of the more difficult concepts of the suffering of change and all-pervasive suffering than they are of the suffering of physical pain. So when they encounter this "lower" type of suffering, it may be more difficult for them to feel compassion.

Why do some people who say they are Buddhists have no compassion?

In Tibet, a grandmother or grandfather who sees a sick and hungry dog will feel sorry for

"THE FAILURE TO
UNDERSTAND EMPTINESS
AND INTERDEPENDENCE
IS IGNORANCE."

"CULTIVATING AWARENESS OF EMPTINESS MEANS THAT IGNORANCE—THE SOURCE OF OUR CONFUSION AND SUFFERING—CAN BE EXTINGUISHED."

it and give it something to eat, while by comparison *some* monks seem to have no compassion.

Here is the personal experience of Geshe Dorje Damdul. He was educated at the Tibet Children's Village School for Tibetan refugees, where he received a modern Western-style education. Then at the age of twenty, he entered our monastery in south India. So he can speak about two distinct educational experiences.

Geshe recognizes that some very knowledgeable monks do not translate what they have learned into practice. On the other hand, there are monks who are truly able to use their academic knowledge to cultivate the mind of compassion. Then their compassion is so transcendent and profound that you cannot compare it with the compassion of ordinary people.

Geshe studied in the monastery for sixteen years, and his personal experience was that monastic life was very different from that of society outside the monastery.

In the monastery you feel so relaxed, and your friends are always there to offer you help. But once you leave that institution, then gradually you feel a huge difference, as though there is no one around you and you have to sustain yourself.

In the monastery there is an enormous amount of harmony, an incredible sense of confidence, security, and happiness.

That's the positive side of it. [Laughs.]

But I do admit there is also a negative side. Among very knowledgeable people in monasteries, some never integrate their knowledge with actual practice, so in spite of all their education and understanding, because of their lack of practice, they may behave in a coldhearted and indifferent way. But there are only a few monks with these negative traits. Most people in the monasteries do integrate study and practice, and many possess deep kindness that is based on wisdom.

In the worst cases, some monks become very learned in monastic institutions, but they are not able to integrate knowledge with practice. They become very eloquent and good at debating other people, so nobody can really challenge them, while in practice they lack compassion and kindness.

Suffering and the Middle Path

The middle path is very important in Buddhism, but it does not simply mean staying in the middle, avoiding extremes.

The Buddha himself was born as a prince into life of worldly pleasure but then renounced the world and went to live as an ascetic, practicing fasting and austerities until he nearly died. But he did not attain enlightenment, so he came out of the forest, healed his mind and body, and then entered into meditation and attained enlightenment.

The middle path means avoiding extremes of pleasure and pain, but it does not mean

"THE MIDDLE PATH DOES NOT

SIMPLY MEAN

STAYING IN THE MIDDLE,

AVOIDING EXTREMES . . .

... THE TRUE MEANING

OF THE MIDDLE PATH

IS MOVING DYNAMICALLY

BETWEEN EXTREMES."

that we should merely remain in the middle from the start.

In Buddhism, the true meaning of the middle way is moving dynamically between the two, experiencing both.

When we are between the two, we are *here*.

So many monks and other Buddhists do not address the actual problem of suffering, but mistakenly think that the middle path means just to sit comfortably in the middle, avoiding extremes, without doing anything.

It is not enought to remain quiety meditating in the monastery—we must confront the suffering in the outside world.

"WHEN WE ARE BETWEEN

THE TWO EXTREMES,

WE ARE *HERE*.**"**

It is foolish to say that the middle path means to be indifferent to reality or not even to know about the other extremes.

The Buddha taught the need for peace. Naturally we may ask why he taught that peace is important.

Why?

We know that violence causes suffering. So we may seek peace because we think that to get rid of that suffering, we must put an end to violence.

We need to have both the Buddha's teachings and the awareness that is based on our own actual experience.

"IF WE LOOK AT THE BUDDHA'S LIFE STORY, IT IS CLEAR WHY HE TAUGHT THE MIDDLE PATH."

If we look at the Buddha's life story, it is clear why he taught the middle path. The Buddha himself taught based on his own experience.

Buddha renounced the world, went off alone to undergo religious training, and practiced austerities for six years.

He often fasted, but he ultimately realized that fasting and other physical efforts were not sufficient. He saw that he had to use his intelligence, so he stopped his ascetic practices and began to eat again.

When he used his intelligence to cultivate wisdom, then, for the first time, he attained enlightenment.

First, we must become aware of suffering. Even without trying to, sooner or later we all experience suffering and want to put an end to it.

To eliminate suffering, we must understand that ascetic physical practices are not enough, but that it is absolutely essential to use our human intelligence to cultivate wisdom.

The Buddha himself taught based on his own experience, and we too must start with our own experience of suffering.

"FOR A HAPPY LIFE,

INNER VALUES ARE

WHAT WE NEED

RIGHT *NOW*."

Love and Attachment

Scientists are already starting to show that inner values [holds hand to his heart] are what matter most for a happy life, and they are what we need right now, not only spiritually but also for our physical well-being.

Our whole society is deluded by material things and has lost sight of what is truly valuable. We judge everything on a material level, and we don't recognize any other values.

In families, too, people who earn money are treated well, and those who don't are treated as useless. People treat their children better if they are likely to earn a lot in the future, and they neglect their children who are not.

Some may even feel that since disabled children are not useful, it would be better to kill them. The same is true of old people—since they don't earn money anymore, they are not treated well and are given nothing but leftovers to eat.

We deal with animals the same way. Hens that lay eggs are treated well, but male chickens are killed. Females that don't lay eggs are also killed. People are exactly the same. Only useful people are valued, and those who are not useful are abandoned.

Our society is youth-oriented, but we can also say that it is use-oriented. Modern civilization recognizes those who are useful but not those who are useless.

In a society that treats only useful people well, we now have to pray that we will live shorter lives. [Puts hands together.] When we get old, we will be useless. [Bursts out laughing.]

This is a global problem. I think most societies believe money is the only way.

Deeper human values and compassionate friends are the most important things in life, but people don't recognize that.

For example, in a poor household that is filled with affection, everybody is happy. But even in a billionaire's household, if the family members are jealous and suspicious and unloving toward each other, then no

"HOW DO WE DISTINGUISH BETWEEN LOVE AND ATTACHMENT? IT IS THE DIFFERENCE BETWEEN DEEPER VALUES AND SUPERFICIAL VALUES."

matter how wealthy they are or how nice their furniture is, they are still unhappy.

This example clearly shows the difference between superficial values and deeper, higher values.

The affection and kindness that we human beings originally possess are the deeper values, the foundation of all human values.

With this foundation, superficial values that have to do with money and material possessions can contribute to human happiness. Without it, those superficial values are meaningless.

How then should we distinguish between love and attachment? Some parents think that having a "good child" is proof that they are loving parents. They believe that if their child gets into a good school, it is because of their love for the child.

Getting into a good school is not a bad thing, of course, but if the parents want the child to get into a good school based on conditional love, isn't that just control that goes by the name of love?

Children are not their parents' property, but when the parents treat them like property, that is attachment not love. It seems they use conditional love to control their children.

They are attached not only to their children, but also to their own image of themselves

"WHEN PARENTS TREAT THEIR CHILDREN LIKE PROPERTY— WHEN THEY VALUE ONLY THEIR ACCOMPLISHMENTS—THAT IS ATTACHMENT NOT LOVE."

as the parents of good children. That kind of relationship is not real love.

This is the difference between conditional love and unconditional love.

I think genuine love will be given absolutely equally to a bright child or a handicapped child alike. In fact, I think a handicapped child would naturally receive more love, more care. But if the love is not genuine, if it is conditional, then a handicapped child would be seen as useless and would not be loved.

To some extent, I think animals also behave like parents with conditional love. Some kinds of birds give more food to the larger

"WE TEND TO
EVALUATE PEOPLE
BASED ON THEIR
USEFULNESS."

offspring in their nests. I noticed that owls and eagles don't feed the same amount to their larger and smaller offspring. Since they feed more to the larger offspring, I thought maybe the smaller offspring would eventually die. Maybe in the animal world they are distinguishing among their offspring in the same way that humans do. I don't know.

With dogs and cats, puppies and kittens, how do the mothers treat the strong versus the weak offspring?

I don't know, but I am very interested in this question. If they are giving more food to the large and strong offspring and not much to their weaker offspring, then they are distinguishing among the value of various offspring. Animals behave in such a way because of biological factors.

Female animals also often prefer males that are larger, so that they will have healthier, stronger offspring. They prefer larger males because of a biological instinct to propagate the species and produce better offspring.

Male deer will often fight over the females, and the one that wins looks majestic while the loser withdraws, looking very disappointed as he leaves. [Laughs.] All these things have a biological basis.

In the same way, if a human mother has several children, treating the stronger child better has a biological origin. And if she sees the weaker child as useless and does not give him very much care—setting aside what we just said about money and a child's value—I wonder if that behavior arises from a biological point of view.

What is Civilization?

If culture is a certain fixed pattern of behavior, then we can say that culture exists in the animal world, but civilization is a little more difficult.

On the animal level, everything is governed by physical factors. On the human level, in ancient times, we were closer to the level of animals, in that physical strength was superior. The physical was all that mattered.

But as civilization advanced, human intelligence became more dominant. Through human intelligence, life has advanced and become more sophisticated, and that social development is what we call civilization.

"THE CONCEPT OF
CIVILIZATION IS
DEEPLY CONNECTED TO
HUMAN VALUES."

In other words, the concept of civilization is deeply connected to human values, or at least to our intelligence. So the triumph of the strong over the weak on a physical level has become less important.

Intelligence is a unique trait that human beings possess, and in civilization the intellectual level is superior to the physical level. Just as human intelligence plays an important role, so also do the true affection and kindness that human beings possess.

The most important basic human values of affection and kindness exist on a different level than the intellect.

"THE MOST IMPORTANT HUMAN VALUES OF AFFECTION AND KINDNESS EXIST ON A DIFFERENT LEVEL THAN THE INTELLECT."

In a civilization founded on the intellectual level, the intellect plays a greater role, and we tend to evaluate and select people based on their usefulness.

But if we make only intellectual judgments and neglect our original attributes of affection and kindness, and instead choose and value only things that are useful, there is a danger that we will leave those judgments as the legacy of our civilization.

I woud like to speak about what I mean when I talk about civilization.

From an animal society in which physical strength was dominant, human intelligence

"CIVILIZATION FOUNDED ON THE INTELLECTUAL LEVEL TENDS TO EVALUATE AND SELECT PEOPLE BASED ON THEIR USEFULNESS."

gave rise to what we call "civilization," which overcame the animalistic law of the jungle.

But because the intellect tends to value things according to their usefulness, a different kind of discrimination arose, and by relying solely on our intellectual judgment, we risk suppressing the affection and kindness that are our most basic attributes as human animals.

However, looking back at human history, it was not always the case that those with the greatest physical strength had the most power.

Human society began as a hunter-gatherer society—it was a perfectly egalitarian

"BY RELYING SOLELY ON OUR INTELLECTUAL JUDGMENT, WE RISK SUPPRESSING THE AFFECTION AND KINDNESS THAT ARE OUR MOST BASIC ATTRIBUTES AS HUMAN ANIMALS."

society. If a hunter brought in game, the game was divided evenly among all members of the community. In fact, this method is the best one to ensure the survival of the whole community.

At that time, of course, meat could not be preserved. So, for example, if I shot a big deer and then kept it only for my own family to consume, some would certainly be left over and go to waste.

So the most logical way for the community to survive is that on days that I shoot game, I distribute it evenly among everyone, and on days when others shoot game, they do the same.

Because hunter-gatherer societies had this method of even distribution, there was almost no differentiation between people who had power and those who didn't.

But the introduction of farming transformed human society. Farming societies stayed in one place, so that people could now store grain that had been harvested, as well as own furniture, household items, and other possessions.

In farming societies, the gap between rich and poor expanded dramatically, and a sharp distinction arose between those who had power and those who did not.

As the accumulation of wealth became possible and vastly powerful institutions were established, the so-called four great ancient civilizations took shape.

The introduction of farming gave rise to the idea of personal property, so that for survival, instead of dividing resources evenly among all members of the community, it was safer for people to accumulate their own personal resources.

Eventually, people began to fight over power and wealth, and these struggles marked the beginning of systematic warfare and conflict.

So one can say that the tendency for the physically strong to dominate the weak did not exist before the advent of civilization.

But this is not entirely so.

I think even within a hunting society, as with animals, the physically stronger animal takes more meat. When a mother lion kills an animal, the father lion swaggers over, drives away everyone else, and enjoys the meat himself. The strong take more. I think the same was true of early human beings.

But then, compared to other animal societies, human beings have a stronger awareness of community. Everyone's life depends on the community.

To a cultural anthropologist, the word "civilization" refers to the four great civilizations surrounding the Nile, Tigris-Euphrates, Indus, and Yellow rivers. There is an assumption that "civilization" did not exist before these societies.

But civilization exists in the animal world. I use the word civilization to refer to the system of individual consciousness and society governed by the intelligence in both animals and humans that transcends their animal nature.

In this case, the hunter-gatherer societies and their practice of equal distribution mark a period of history in which a balance existed between the intellect and the basic human values of affection and kindness.

Four or five million years ago, monkeys came down from the trees and began to walk upright and thus took a step toward becoming human.

These first humans were called Pithecanthropus, and they were followed by the primitive humans represented by the Peking man and Java man, while human beings today are descended from Cro-Magnon Man.

These categories do not imply a linear evolution, but they do give a general view of that process.

"CIVILIZATION IS THE SYSTEM
OF INDIVIDUAL CONSCIOUSNESS
AND SOCIETY GOVERNED BY THE
INTELLIGENCE IN BOTH ANIMALS
AND HUMANS THAT TRANSCENDS
THEIR ANIMAL NATURE."

The hunter-gatherer societies I spoke about were already composed of Cro-Magnon Man, whose livelihood was hunting and gathering.

The age that anthropologists call "pre-civilization," in which the animal level dominated, corresponds to the age of Pithecanthropus and the primitive humans who followed them. Certainly in the sense that those societies used fire and tools, they were already set apart from wild animals, but human beings were still very animal-like.

After that stage, however, human consciousness evolved rapidly. The brain developed, and brain capacity reached that of human beings today, which led to the awakening of the intellect.

For example, when the remains of one of the now-extinct Neanderthal were excavated, it was discovered that he had been living for years with a broken leg. Even though he was disabled, friends had helped him. The age of helping each other had begun.

This period was also revolutionary because the concept of death first arose within human beings. They began to bury their dead. They became conscious of death and the world after death. This awareness was also the discovery of "life."

To become conscious of death was to become conscious that they were living life, which was not death. As we came to perceive the basic distinction between life and death, we became more aware that we were alive. The intellect is based on the consciousness that makes distinctions, and the most basic of those is the distinction between life and death.

For a long time, Neanderthal man was believed to be the direct ancestor of the human race, but genetic analysis has disproved this idea. The dominant theory now is that Neanderthal man died out because they could not adapt to various environmental changes.

Either way, during this period, the intellect began to develop in human beings, and they moved beyond the stage in which the strong dominated the weak. Hunter-gatherer societies were based on mutual help and even distribution of resources.

To sum up this history of the human race, the "civilization" I speak of is a period when human beings transcended the dominance of strong over weak, and they came to possess the intellect, but still held onto the basic attributes of affection and kindness.

With the shift to a farming society, however, people planted seeds in spring and harvested crops in autumn, and thus became

"THE INTELLECT IS BASED ON THE CONSCIOUSNESS THAT MAKES DISTINCTIONS, AND THE MOST BASIC DISTINCTION IS BETWEEN LIFE AND DEATH."

aware of time. Being aware of time means not living in the here and now.

As the intellect became dominant, people increasingly made distinctions based on usefulness, and the intellectual violence of those who killed others in their quest for wealth and power became acceptable.

Yet farming societies still had a powerful sense of community, which suppressed the maladies caused by the intellect.

With the rise of industrial societies, however, the power of the community declined, and people forgot that they were social animals.

Because we mistakenly began to see ourselves as individuals living separate lives, it was no longer possible to stop the reckless domination of the intellect.

Then our most basic human attributes of affection and kindness became obscured.

"INTELLECTUAL CAPACITY HAS
PRODUCED CIVILIZATION,
BUT IT HAS ALSO BROUGHT US
A LOT OF SUFFERING."

Love and Innate Healing Power

We are not merely animals, but animals that possess an intellect; this intellectual capacity has produced civilization, but it has also brought us a lot of suffering.

Most of our spiritual problems are due to our very sophisticated intelligence and powerful imagination. Science and technology have also given us unlimited hopes. As a result, we sometimes forget our basic nature as human beings.

Our basic nature as human beings comes from our basic nature as mammals.

"MOST OF OUR SPIRITUAL

PROBLEMS ARE DUE TO

OUR VERY SOPHISTICATED

INTELLIGENCE AND POWERFUL

IMAGINATION."

"AS A RESULT, WE SOMETIMES FORGET OUR BASIC NATURE AS HUMAN BEINGS."

Let's take the modern medical system as an example. When a person is sick, Tibetan medicine generally seeks to bring forth the body's inherent natural healing power. But Western surgical procedures seek to cut out the part of the body that is not working, as though repairing a machine.

Once a machine breaks, it cannot repair itself. So with a machine, the broken part must be taken out and thrown away.

But our bodies are not machines. Even if the human body is damaged, sick, or hurt, it has the inherent natural power to heal itself.

When we rely too much on modern science and technology, our lifestyle itself becomes like a machine, and we move away from our basic human nature.

A person who has become like a machine has no room left to cultivate affection or compassion for others. We are all knowledge, but we lack compassion.

When we cooperate with each other, when we are connected through mutual trust, when we are filled with love and compassion, the immune system is strong.

But when others betray us or we feel neglected, when we feel angry and sad at the way others have treated us, the power of our immune system declines dramatically.

The feeling of loneliness combined with powerlessness weakens the immune system more than anything else.

When we feel alone and abandoned but cannot do anything about it, when love and compassion have abandoned us, the body's defenses are at their lowest.

Then we can get sick easily, or an illness like cancer that the immune system has been keeping in check can surge out of control.

Science has already shown that our mental and physical health are deeply connected.

This is a very powerful argument for the importance of peace of mind, compassion, and kindness.

"WHEN WE RELY TOO MUCH ON MODERN TECHNOLOGY, OUR LIFESTYLE ITSELF BECOMES LIKE A MACHINE . . .

... AND WE MOVE AWAY FROM OUR

BASIC HUMAN NATURE."

In an industrialized society like Japan, it is not sufficient to study Buddhist teachings and texts. We need efforts to link those teachings to scientific knowledge.

Fear, anxiety, and stress weaken the immune system. Some scientists have actually described the anger as eating our immune functions.

On the other hand, a relaxed state of compassion and kindness brings us inner peace and supports and augments the function of the immune system.

These scientific facts demonstrate the importance of inner values to people in modern society.

"WE MUST REALIZE HOW
IMPORTANT THESE VALUES ARE
AND MAKE THE EFFORT TO
CULTIVATE THEM."

These inner values cannot be produced by medicine, injections, or machines.

The only way is for us to realize how important these values are and to make the effort to cultivate them.

The important thing now is to investigate these ideas in our own mental laboratory, especially whatever has to do with the emotions.

For that purpose, the Buddhist tradition offers very rich resources. Buddhism categorizes the different emotions and explains in detail how to deal with negative emotions and increase positive ones. Then Buddhism becomes relevant in our daily life.

Buddhism for a Modern World

Buddhism is not just about chanting sutras but is also connected to the scientific knowledge we just spoke of, about the connection between the immune system and an inner state of kindness.

But what is the meaning of Buddhism today, and how can it be made relevant for modern society? It must not remain a closed religious world but must be brought into daily life.

There is a saying, "Whatever you do, if it is not accompanied by enlightenment then no matter how many mantras you chant, you will be reborn as a snake."

"THE MIND OF ENLIGHTENMENT IS NOT MERE KNOWLEDGE BUT AN INNATE MENTAL QUALITY."

The mind of enlightenment is not mere knowledge but an innate mental quality. We feel and experience it deep within ourselves.

Ceremonies, prayers, mantras, and chanting sutras are not sufficient. Reciting the Heart Sutra in itself is no different from playing a tape recorder [laughs] if it is not accompanied by the enlightened mind.

There are certainly unenlightened priests who chant like tape recorders. Some people say that reciting the Heart Sutra has magical powers, and they really do feel that the sounds of the sutra's words hold something mysterious.

"RECITING THE HEART SUTRA IN ITSELF IS NO DIFFERENT FROM PLAYING A TAPE RECORDER IF IT IS NOT ACCOMPANIED BY THE ENLIGHTENED MIND."

I think in some special circumstances, just hearing the sound itself has good effects. But would it help animals, too? Even if an animal did not have the karma for it to produce good effects, do you think that listening to the sutra would help him?

To become a tathāgata [literally, "thus come one," an epithet for a Buddha], one must have accumulated both virtue and wisdom. Both must be there. It is the same thing.

To bring Buddhism to life, we must have a Buddhist revival. To do that, Buddhism must be thoroughly explained on the basis of scientific research. I think that's the proper way to do it.

"TO BECOME A BUDDHA,
ONE MUST HAVE ACCUMULATED
BOTH VIRTUE AND WISDOM."

First, the Buddhist community should have a deeper knowledge of how the Buddhist system works. And then this practice should be thoroughly researched according to scientific findings, so that it becomes real and convincing.

Then monks should guide other people in the study of Buddhism.

That is why the monks themselves must first pay more attention to the importance of study.

Through religious practice, the monks should serve as examples of good human beings.

If the monks can truly be examples for others, then people will be led to study and practice Buddhism.

So these changes are nothing new. This is not reform but revival.

Self-Responsibility

Guru yoga is very important in the Tibetan tradition, but one negative aspect of it is that guru yoga emphasizes the attitude of entrusting everything to the guru, which leads to the danger of too much dependence on the guru.

Someone once asked me what it means to take refuge [in the Three Treasures of Buddhism: the Buddha, dharma, and sangha].

The question was whether taking refuge means to become perfectly dependent on something, to lose your independence.

"IN BUDDHISM, WE ASPIRE TO BECOME

LIKE BUDDHA OURSELVES,

AND IN THAT ACT,

INDIVIDUAL PRIDE IS VERY STRONG,

AND WE DO NOT BECOME DEPENDENT."

But in Buddhism, especially in the Mahāyāna tradition, taking refuge means that we aspire to become like Buddha ourselves, and in that act, individual pride is very strong, and we do not become dependent.

In religions that accept the existence of God, however, everything is created and determined by God. God is great, but I am nothing.

In that way of thinking, the self cannot act autonomously, because we are perfectly dependent on the creator God, and God determines everything.

This way of thinking is very useful for some people, but from a Buddhist point of view, it discourages people from having self-

"THE BUDDHA TAUGHT THAT ULTIMATELY YOU YOURSELF SHOULD BECOME A BUDDHA. AND HE HIMSELF WAS ONCE AN ORDINARY PERSON LIKE US."

confidence, pride, the creative power to accomplish things.

The Buddha taught that ultimately you yourself should become a Buddha. And he himself was once an ordinary person like us. He set an example for us by practicing until he attained Buddhahood.

BEING HERE

Afterword

Commenetary by Noriyuki Ueda

During my interview with the Dalai Lama, I realized for the first time what it meant that he was the living embodiment of Avalokiteśvara and why he exists in the first place.

It is well known that the Dalai Lama reincarnates in successive human forms. When a Dalai Lama passes away, a search party forms to look for the next Dalai Lama, and they travel all over Tibet seeking the child that is his next incarnation. The fourteenth Dalai Lama was discovered at the age of three as the reincarnation of the thirteenth

Dalai Lama. The reincarnating Dalai Lama is also the embodiment of Avalokiteśvara. When Avalokiteśvara's life as a human being ends, he appears again in a different human form.

From my Japanese point of view, all this sounds exotic, and for Westerners even more so.

When I first met the Dalai Lama in person at an international conference many years ago, the Western participants there gazed at him with a fascination for the "mystery of the East" that he represented to them.

But why does the Dalai Lama reincarnate? Why does Avalokiteśvara bodhisattva mani-

"WHY DOES THE DALAI LAMA REINCARNATE?"

fest himself? Many people say it is because Tibetan society believes in reincarnation. All living things reincarnate, and so does the Dalai Lama, so do bodhisattvas.

But only the Buddha escapes the cycle of birth and death. Life is suffering, and reincarnation is the continuation of suffering. Only the Buddha escapes rebirth and suffering and attains the liberation of nirvana.

Yet Avalokiteśvara reincarnates because he wants to.

Avalokiteśvara is the bodhisattva who vows to Amida Buddha that he will save all sentient beings. He is the bodhisattva who saves sentient beings for countless eons

"THE DALAI LAMA IS THE
BODHISATTVA WHO VOWS
TO AMIDA BUDDHA
THAT HE WILL SAVE
ALL BEINGS FROM SUFFERING."

until at last he attains enlightenment and Amida invites him to become a Buddha.

But Avalokiteśvara turns down that offer. He says, "I want to be attached to helping sentient beings. I will not become a Buddha, I will keep coming back as a bodhisattva until I have saved all beings from suffering.

"Instead of attaining liberation and becoming a Buddha, I want to keep being reborn and saving sentient beings . . ."

The Dalai Lama is not simply being reborn. The bodhisattva's will to save sentient beings from suffering is manifested in the form of the Dalai Lama. He emphasizes positive attachment that is worth keeping, because he himself is the manifestation of Avalokiteśvara's own attachment.

Without the attachment to saving all sentient beings, the Dalai Lama would not exist.

That will is what gives birth to the Dalai Lama. There is a will that precedes birth and death. There is a will that precedes existence. That is what a bodhisattva is.

But Avalokiteśvara does not merely reincarnate so that he can inherit an old tradition.

To save sentient beings, Buddhism must change with the times. A bodhisattva must strive to continuously learn, learn, learn. He must deeply study the old traditions as well as modern society and modern science.

"A BODHISATTVA

MUST STRIVE TO

CONTINUOUSLY LEARN,

LEARN, LEARN."

"HE MUST SEEK WAYS FOR
TRADITIONAL BUDDHIST TEACHINGS
TO MEET THE DEMANDS
OF MODERN SOCIETY."

He must seek ways for traditional Buddhist teachings to meet the demands of modern society, and he must continually investigate the role of Buddhism in his own time. If he does not, he cannot really save anyone.

The Dalai Lama himself must feel deeply how powerless Buddhism is when it does not keep up with the times, how powerless a bodhisattva is when he cannot address the society in which he lives.

This is how he describes his youth in Tibet in *Freedom in Exile: The Autobiography of the Dalai Lama* (New York: HarperCollins, 1991):

> Of course, whilst I lived in Tibet, being Dalai Lama meant a great deal. It meant

that I lived a life far removed from the toil and discomfort of the vast majority of my people. Everywhere I went, I was accompanied by a retinue of servants. I was surrounded by government ministers and advisors clad in sumptuous silk robes, men drawn from the most exalted and aristocratic families in the land. My daily companions were brilliant scholars and highly realized religious adepts.

When he was a child, regents who were sometimes corrupt or sought personal benefit held the real political power, and because they lacked foresight and ignored the revolution that had occurred, they ended up allowing the Chinese invasion to happen.

Buddhist teachings could not stop the invasion either.

This sense of powerlessness is expressed clearly in the Dalai Lama's autobiography.

No matter how profound a teaching is, if it does not keep up with the times, it has no power to help those who are suffering.

The Dalai Lama must have felt powerless, but he did not allow that feeling to dominate him. As Avalokiteśvara, what could he do to alleviate human suffering? At that time, he cast off the husk of the person he had been until then.

"NO MATTER HOW PROFOUND
A TEACHING IS, IF IT DOES NOT
KEEP UP WITH THE TIMES,
IT HAS NO POWER TO HELP
THOSE WHO ARE SUFFERING."

He stopped reigning from the top of a pyramid, where the only people he spoke with were those who worshiped him.

To test out the logic of Buddhist teachings, he began to have discussions on an equal footing with scientists, politicians, and other religious leaders.

He put himself in situations where he might lose arguments, as he groped for what role Buddhism could play in the world.

That approach is exactly the opposite of the attitude of religious people who also feel powerless but never engage in debate unless they are sure to win and be able to show off.

Buddhism was not there to feed the Dalai Lama's power, but only to help humanity.

When we hear that the Dalai Lama is the living embodiment of Avalokiteśvara, we tend to think that idea belongs to an old, outdated tradition.

Yet it is because the Dalai Lama is the embodiment of Avalokiteśvara that he is on the cutting edge of modern society.

When he visited Stanford University in 2005, he spent one day of his three-day program there in a symposium with pioneering neuroscientists from the medical school, engaged in a wide-ranging discussion with them on the topic of how desire, attachment, and suffering arise. The Dalai Lama actively engages in dialogues with today's leaders all over the world.

His lifetime of over eighty years spans feudal times, modernity, and post-modernity. He was raised as a feudal monarch, yet in exile he has promoted the modernization of politics and religion.

In place of the coldness of the modern social system, he advocates a society that is based on affection and kindness.

This affection and kindness does not merely represent a revival of traditional values. It is not a movement to restore what has been lost, but to manifest the affection and kindness that have developed in the wake of modernization that are right for our times.

Avalokiteśvara, whose life spans feudal to post-modern times, is none other than the Dalai Lama himself.

He is here, now.

Titles in This Series

Be Happy

Be Angry

Be Here

Be Kind

About the Author

His Holiness the fourteenth Dalai Lama, Tenzin Gyatso, is the spiritual and temporal leader of the Tibetan people. He has written a number of books on Buddhism and philosophy and has received many international awards, including the 1989 Nobel Peace Prize.

Hampton Roads Publishing Company

. . . for the evolving human spirit

Hampton Roads Publishing Company
publishes books on a variety of subjects,
including spirituality, health, and other
related topics.

For a copy of our latest trade catalog, call
(978) 465-0504 or visit our distributor's
website at *www.redwheelweiser.com*. You
can also sign up for our newsletter and
special offers by going to
www.redwheelweiser.com/newsletter.